ABIOLA SABA LLC
P. O. BOX 352
MULLICA HILL
NJ 08062

Telephone: 856-264-4480
Email: SABA@ABIOLASABA.COM
Website: WWW.ABIOLASABA.COM/INNERWINNER

All Scriptures used are taken from Holy Bible, The Good News Translation. Used with permission.

Editor: Angie Bruce. Hertfordshire, England
Page design: Rainbow Creative Group (1-205-259-8758)
Cover design: fiverr.com/alerrandre

Publisher: ABSAB PUBLISHING
ISBN: 978-0-9915864-1-7

The Inner Winner
Unleashed

The toughest challenge of my life has led to my biggest inspiration

ABIOLA SABA

Be prepared to leap to the top, and I'll see you there!!!

To my mother, Mrs. Dupe Owodunni. Mother dearest, you put your life on hold for us to have ours. Mother, you taught us about the love of God. Your demonstration of that love makes me appreciate God even more. Thank you for your agape love.

Advance Praises

"A very inspiring book which shows you how one can overcome our daily fears, circumstances and challenges to reach our goals against all odds!!"
Subramanian Narayan, Renergetics Consulting
Singapore, Singapore

"Abiola. You are authentic and true to your conviction that pain and seeming defeat can be turned into victory. You have lived this truth, and now you teach others to do the same. You are an inspiration, a voice of courage and encouragement to this generation. I celebrate you on the release of your first book and look forward to the timeless testimonies and stories that will come from its readers."
Peter Akindeji Coker
Lagos, Nigeria

"Abiola, I love the spirit of Boldness, humility and courage in which your faith has made you. You stand for your life, your family and God's purpose for your life. You transcend your life with inspiration, and courage for many people around the world. This is a true communicator of God's Purpose for humanity. Thank you for feeding my life with courage and Faith."
Martha Loaisiga
Melbourne, Vic. Australia

"Abiola Saba, A WOMAN who's aim is to inspire those with great inspiration by imparting her knowledge. Her success will always follow her, because she includes GOD in her carrier."
Samuel Cleare
Nassau City, New Providence, Bahamas

"God has a unique plan for everyone of us. For Abiola, she has gained a much fruitful life through Lou and now she shares her story to inspire and encourage people. What a way to glorify God!"
Corinne Lau Certified Coach, Speaker and Trainer
Hong Kong

"I believe strongly that two things are a great fuel for success, one Inspiration and two, information both of which I have found in every single page of this book " THE INNER WINNER UNLEASHED". Thank you Abiola for taking a sad personal experience and turning it into inspiration for the world. In this work many will find that truly there is an inner strength waiting for anyone who is ready to tap into."
Derric Yuh Ndim. Co-founder at Peak Performance Consulting Unlockingyourtruepotential.com
Johannesburg, South Africa

"Life sometimes throws curve balls at us? Do we learn from them and grow or do we wallow and fade away? Abiola chose the former. I know after reading this, your life will never be the same again. This is indeed a book long coming and I am glad it finally came through. May you find much inspiration as I did knowing this silent giant, with a heart of gold and the love and fear of GOD. Abiola is indeed a warrior for GOD!!!!!"
Anthonia Ngafor, Physician in training/Mentor/Speaker/ Coach
Chicago, USA

"Abiola, I believe in YOU. You have tapped in to what Napoleon Hill refers to as Infinite Intelligence. Thank you for investing the time to write your story. It is one that must be told. Yours in success."
Trish Buzzone, Founding Partner, Certified Coach, Speaker and Teacher
Florida, USA

"'Inner Winner Unleashed' has further corroborated an adage which says it is not what happens to you in life that counts but how you react to it. Through this book, the author has been able to show us how we can turn our challenges to opportunities. Thank you Mrs. Saba for this inspirational piece, you remain a gift to this generation."
Temitope Omotayo, Inspirational Writer and Speaker, Author of "Unleashing Your Talent"
Michigan, USA

"When I met Abiola Saba she was in Nigeria training on Cardiopulmonary Resuscitation. What drew me to this woman was her warm personality, a willingness to share what she knew, her patience, and long suffering at ensuring a life was saved through the techniques she was trying to impart. Little did I know that she had been going through a lot, caring for her son who at that time had special needs. Upon interacting with her after the training session we shared a lot of life experiences and I came away thinking "what an inestimable jewel". Her husband is truly blessed to have a wife like her and so are her children to have such a warm caring, loving mother and friend. She had strength of purpose, focus, courage and determination to shine her light to anyone who needed it and drew her inspiration and deep seated wisdom from her Maker, Creator Redeemer and Friend!! Abiola my message to you is keep excelling, keep focused, you have found your life assignment, do what you have to do to help others discover their INNER WINNER and UNLEASH IT!! Blessedness!"
Eniola Prosper Afolabi
Lagos, Nigeria

"Abiola's self-confidence, internal drive and self-motivation has always been supported by her passion and professional life which translates into a deep willingness to helping others fulfill their purpose in life."
Peter Oluremi Osinubi
Delaware, USA

"Abiola shares with us how we can cope with difficult times and strategies to stay strong at all times... as she rightly said "You cannot judge your life by your circumstances; otherwise you may lose in the battle of life". Keep this book close to you and live an inspired life! Thank you for sharing this with the world. You are a blessing."
Bernard Kevin Clive, Amazon best-selling author
Accra, Ghana

"This book is Abiola's way of helping people move past a place of unhappiness to discerning their inner winner; to see and have hope, perseverance and aspiration in whatever happens to them in life."
Akintokunbo A Adejumo, Affinity Libra Ltd Global Coordinator, Champions For Nigeria
London, England

"Praise God for the success of this powerful book. I believe that God will continue to use you to change the lives of the people like me and many more around the world."
Hercules Palme
Jim Papua, New Guinea

Acknowledgments

I am thankful and grateful to God. You indeed are my God. You stood by me, You promised to comfort me, and You did. Way beyond my expectation. I was not born qualified, but through the toughest challenge of my life, You qualified me to reach out to millions, to encourage, inspire, motivate and challenge millions to unleash the Inner Winner within. Oh what a wonderful Savior. Even when situations did not make sense, trusting God's heart towards us made perfect sense. To God alone be the glory.

To my husband, and children, God is The super glue that holds us together. I love you dearly.

Olaoluwa, my son, you have inspired me, making me a better person. Before you came, life was about me, myself, and I, my attitude was a selfish one then. Now I am wiser because you came into my life. You brought the best out of me. I am so thankful for your life. I miss you dearly, but I am thankful you came. Continue to rest in peace Lou bobo, my only September baby.

To everyone who stood by us, in the toughest challenge of our lives, may God open the book of remembrance to you and your family.

All my family, friends and fans, I appreciate you more than you can ever know. Thank you for your prayers, love and support.

Foreword

The motivation behind this book is very personal not only to Abiola, but also to all those who know her from all aspects of life. Abiola's son Lou was called back home by our Almighty Father in 2011 at the age of 8 years. Lou was special in every imaginable way. His uniqueness captivated our love and we miss him dearly.

The memories that I have of Lou are numerous, but one that many can attest to, is that he always smelt so good (a mixture of Lavender and Chamomile). The scent and presence of Lou created an atmosphere of calmness, warmth and love in the room. There was always a great sense of positive energy around him that makes one emerge fully charged with courage and motivation.

These aspects of Lou are what ignited Abiola's passion as a motivational speaker. Her mission is to give all that she can to others and to share her experience so that you may truly live harmoniously in the way in which Lou taught us to live.

The beauty about our beloved son is that it was a journey travelled by many and not just the immediate family. So I am thrilled that Abiola has chosen to write this book.

Abiola, started this journey of being an inspirational leader long before she realized it. Her Inner Winner has always been there, however, a monumental experience in her life unleashed and launched her calling all in one whirl wind.

There is no stopping her now and you will see what I mean as you turn the pages of this book. Since then she has worked with many men and women globally, helping them to find their inner winners through seminars, radio talk shows, web broadcast, distributions of recorded messages, mentorship, as a Keynote speaker at functions and now through her first book "Inner Winner Unleashed".

Her message is always one of encouragement, inspiration and challenge to move her mentees to the next level.

Dr. Nim Sonaike
New Jersey, USA

Table of Contents

Table of Contents

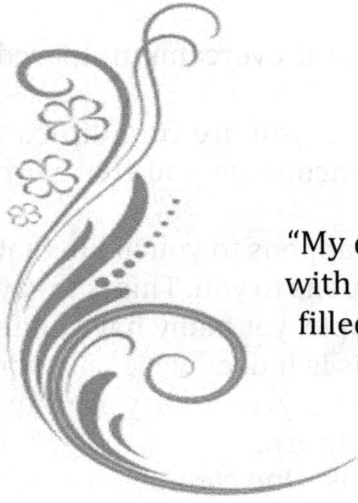

Introduction

"My deepest hope is that rather than filled with sadness that Lou is gone, I want to be filled with inspiration that will create significance in millions of lives."
– Abiola Saba

Whenever I share the experience about my son, people ask me when I am going to write a book about it. As you can tell, I am finally answering the question. This book is long overdue. I have known for some time that a book will come out of our experience.

As much as I desire to write the book, I felt overwhelmed with emotions of missing my son whenever I start writing. Without strength from my Maker, I would not have been able to complete this book. I realized that I had to put my emotions aside so I can be a blessing to others. I give God the glory for all the contents of this book.

You cannot judge your life by your circumstances; otherwise you may lose in the battle of life. It was hard, it was painful, yet, I had to do a mind shift to be supported by heaven. I had to trust God even when situations did not make sense. The trusting led to the gates of heaven being open for endless supply and recovering. Through the toughest challenge of my life, I developed resilience, more wisdom, maturity and became a better person. The challenge I faced and overcame prepared my heart for the future.

May you be blessed and above all, if you are in a difficult chapter of your life, may this book encourage you that with God, there is much hope.

It has been said that it is not what happens to you in life that counts; it is your reaction to what happens to you. This is to say that bad things have happened to people, yet many have gone to do great things with their lives. This is indeed very true, for life's challenges are not supposed to paralyze us; they are supposed to help us discover who we really are.

In addition, life is like writing a book. One cannot get stuck on one page because of disappointment, the next chapter needs to be written as the book is not yet completed.

This book is about discovering an Inner Winner that resides in all of us. The Inner Winner can help us through any situation we find ourselves. However, we have to discover that Inner Winner for it to work for us.

My desire through writing this book is that people move beyond their emotional hurt and fulfill the purpose of their creation. Having gone through my experience, I encourage you to take inspired action, regardless of what has happened to you or in you. You are a champion, who has been created to succeed.

I am excited for the true testimony that whenever God is involved in a thing, He makes it better. For God took my pain and gave me His power; took my hurt and gave me healing; took my test and turned it to an international testimony. Took my failing and gave me His success.

I hope this book motivates, inspires and encourages you to achieve your purpose regardless of what life has thrown in your path. Like Jim Rohm said, result is the name of the game. After reading this book, regardless of the pit you have found yourself, my hope is that you will be inspired to achieve your desired result.

The greatest testimony is yours and I look forward to listening to it.

Your Success, My Assignment!!!
Abiola Saba

CHAPTER 1
Lou My Angel

Looking back at that day, it was a Monday morning. I could hear myself yelling my son, my son, my son noooooooooo. I was in shock; my entire body was in shock. I could hear myself screaming loud. I could feel the shock going through my entire being. Nooooooo, oh my son, my son, my son. In my shock, I was rolling on the floor, yes rolling on the floor. My screaming woke the children up. My second son came out of his room with his hands held up, he was ready to fight. Oh no, my son, my son, my son. Nothing could calm me down, I was scared for me. The pain was unbelievable going through my entire body. Nothing, absolutely nothing made sense at that moment.

Suddenly, I opened my eyes, in my sorrow and saw my daughter rolling on the floor, crying. I thought in my head,

> "Blessed are those who mourn. They will be comforted."
> – Matthew 5:4

why is this girl rolling on the floor? It suddenly dawned on me that in my distress and shock, I had been rolling on the floor. My daughter, on hearing that her brother, our baby son had died suddenly at the age of 8 years, in her shock too, rolled on the floor with me. Then out of nowhere, I heard a whisper in my heart, the same whisper I heard many years back. "I WILL COMFORT YOU, I WILL COMFORT YOU,

> "Sometimes you don't realize your own strength until you come face to face with your greatest weakness."
> – Susan Gale

I WILL COMFORT YOU" Suddenly, like a heavy weight was lifted off my head, I felt light. In my hour of greatest distress, I found great comfort in my Inner Winner and continuously receive inspiration and help. I am grateful, I am thankful, I am happy for You said; You will not leave your children comfortless. Oh what a wonderful Father.

The only option I had was to trust that Voice. The other sorrowful option gave me so much pain that I felt I was going to die. I have to trust this Voice to take me to a place of comfort. I got up, looked at my daughter, pulled her up and said "Des, we will be fine".

This book is an attempt to communicate and accept our humanity. The toughest challenge of my life led to my biggest inspiration. Life dealt my son some terrible blows. How can life be so unfair? I lived for almost a year in the why me stage. I had many pity parties. Unfortunately I was the only one attending it.

I could not understand why life could be so unfair I would murmur. My son Olaoluwa, in Yoruba language meaning God's gift was indeed an answer to our prayers. We called him Lou for short. He was our baby son, so loved, so wanted, and so adored. Our daughter had prayed for a baby sister to play with and share life with. Everyone in the family wanted an addition. At the time, I was busy with my career, and not willing to slow down, so every time that topic came up, I would always answer with "we'll see". When I found

> "The husband who decides to surprise his wife is often very much surprised himself."
> – Voltaire

out I was pregnant with Lou, I became very excited. I found out with this pregnancy, that God sure has a good sense of humor.

Many times, when I celebrate my birthday, friends and family will call from all over the world to wish me a happy birthday. My husband for some reason never remembered my birthday. He even complained and asks why everybody is calling me on such days. I used to get so angry and wondered why he forgets my important day. By the time he remembers, it is late at night and he is trying to make up. Usually, at that time I was too upset to appreciate any birthday greetings or treats from him.

The funny part of my husband's memory is that our three children, if you wake him up from a deep sleep and ask when the birthdays of the three children are, he will give all the dates and may even add the times they were born. Oh how I used to get so upset, I could not figure out why this was so. For many years, he forgot my birthday and only tried to make up when it was obvious that he did not remember. Also, every year I would get mad at him and he would promise to remember the following year only to forget and try to make up again.

When this started affecting me negatively, I started praying that God should please intervene. Yes, God sure has a good sense of humor and nothing is too small for Him to do. So Lou our beloved son was born on the eve of my birthday. Yes, since my husband's memory was good enough to remember all his children's birthday, Lou came as a reminder for my birthday. After Lou was born, my husband never forgets my birthday ever again. Thank You Lord.

A few months after Lou was born, my husband noticed that Lou did not look at him. My daughter and I were the two closest people to Lou at that time and felt my husband just needed to spend more time with Lou. See, we both would say, Lou is looking at us. But as weeks turned into months, we noticed that something was different about our Lou. Anytime we put Lou in his crib, he stayed in the same position. He would not roll to the right or the left. We also noticed that instead of tracking with his look, his attention was more spaced out than looking. We realized something was not right.

I became really angry. I grieved, I blamed, shut the world out. I could not function. I was angry. I questioned God, I asked why God would allow such a thing to happen. I thought even people on drugs have healthy children sometimes. I felt justified that since I did not do any of these, no negative thing should happen to my child.

As angry as I was, I did not get answers. I started wondering why the righteous suffer. Needless say the people around me were not helpful. They did not know how to deal with me, so they just avoided me. Some of our so-called friends were also ignorant. They would greet the other children but stay away from Lou as if what he had was contagious. That left me really hurt. We started the elimination process; the friends who were not adding to us were immediately deleted from our lives.

Worrying about things beyond one's control can lead to illness. Through my experience, I have come to understand that hard times unleash the Inner Winner. We cannot control the hands we are dealt, only how we play the cards. My attitude to this situation will determine my outlook.

Those were my defining moments. I realized I had to work myself out of the negative emotional state of mind, but how do I do that?

I refuse to be bitter. I wanted so much to cultivate optimism. I will build on the good instead of letting my negative emotions run my life; I will make myself too happy to even allow a troubled mind. I have to be strong to take care of Lou and continue to maintain great peace of mind for myself and the rest of the family. I will hold on to hope even when doctors say it is hopeless. I will not let what I can't control prevent me from things that depend on me. I refuse to let the past hold my life hostage. Negative happenings will not color my life permanently. I refuse to break down, I will break through, and I refuse to have any pity party. I will go past this pain, no bitterness from me. The situation will not in any way hold me down, for I am a champion. As much as I desired all these, I was angry and refused to pray.

My Creator saw these inner desires and responded. One day, I had a dream. In my dream I met with Christ. As soon as I saw Christ, I remembered that I had been angry for some time and had refused to pray. Naturally, I was expecting Christ to turn His back on me.

The worldly standard is as you lay your bed, so you lie on it. But the Godly standard is rise up and walk, for your sins are forgiven. Worldly standard is if you refuse to speak with a friend for some time, and the friend sees you, she will probably ignore you too. This was the reaction I expected, but was I wrong.

Instead of a cold reaction, Christ gave me a big smile, had His hands wide opened and bid me to come to Him. I did. I had my head on His chest and cried. Christ wiped the tears away and whispered into my ears, loud and clear." I will comfort you, I will comfort you, I will comfort you. After these reassuring words, Christ then told me that with the same comfort He is using to comfort me, I should go encourage, inspire, and motivate millions to righteousness.

I did not have a clue on what to do with these instructions, but when I woke up that morning, I stood in front of the mirror and said moving forward, I will not be moved by what I see, what I hear, or what they say. I will stay connected with God. While in front of the mirror, I had my moment of decision. I looked at myself and said I do not care what package my son came as, I will love him and take excellent care of him.

I also promised myself that if this happened to put my family and I in the pit, it will be the reason why we will get to the palace. I was determined that through this situation, the world will hear our story as we will testify to the goodness of God in our lives. This testimony will be published to encourage, inspire and motivate millions all over the world.

Anthony Robbins the motivational speaker said, either inspiration or desperation will push a person to action. For me I had both. My inspiration came from meeting with the Maker and my desperation was seeing what my son went through, it inspired me to want to do more.

> "God is our refuge and strength, a very present help in trouble."
> – Psalm 46

The day I had the dream was a Sunday. In my household then, my husband was always the first person to wake up on Sundays and then he wakes the family up for church. That day,

I woke up really happy and also woke my family up for church. They looked at me with surprise. I radiated so much joy that I created a joyous atmosphere. I had been sad for so long and the difference was clear that I was happy. That day when I got to church, I danced like I never danced before. Many were wondering what got into me in a positive way, they were happy that I was happy. Many even hugged me; they were so happy for me.

When we got home, I shared my dream with the family. I also told them that we are heading to the palace for God has wiped off all our tears and fear. Oh what joyous feelings we all experienced. This can only be from God.

Weeks later, I started my affirmation. This will make me bigger and better, I will use this as a training point, it hurts but I will turn it to breakthrough for my family and me. Connecting to my spirituality was a good foundation that got me prepared for the journey ahead.

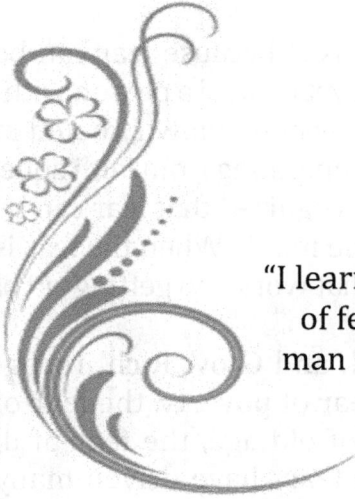

CHAPTER 2
Transcending Fear

"I learned that courage was not the absence of fear, but the triumph over it. The brave man is not he who does not feel afraid, but he who conquers that fear."
— Nelson Mandela

Truth be told, we are all afraid of something. Many generations have experienced fear in one way or another. Fear dates back to the story of Adam and Eve after their deception by the serpent, they were afraid and hid themselves from God. Fear is not a bad thing, depending on the circumstances that surrounds the fear. For example, if you go for a walk in the woods, and see a bear walking your way, your instinct tells you there is danger; you become afraid and probably start running. Fear is a state of mind and does not necessarily have to be an enemy.

Many times, man's action is fear based and not faith based. Sometimes, it is hard for the person to know they

> "I am the LORD your God; I strengthen you and tell you, 'Do not be afraid; I will help you."
> – Isaiah 41:13

are operating from the state of fear. This is because fear can be rooted in a person's subconscious mind, yet control a person without them knowing. Such was my fear, fear of unknown, rooted in my subconscious mind while I felt I was operating from faith zone. Towards the end of that experience, I recognized that fear can be a filler that the enemy uses to occupy the mind. When the fear is identified, it should be filled with faith that works on getting rid of such fear.

Napoleon Hill, the author of 'Think and Grow Rich', recognized some basic fears of men. The fear of poverty, the fear of criticism, the fear of death, the fear of old age, the fear of ill health, the fear of loss of love. These fears have driven many to making some emotional decisions. Some of such fears have created worries and emotional based actions. Underlying fears including the ones in our subconscious mind do manifest in the actions we take. Search yourself carefully as you examined these fears. Do not be quick to dismiss that none are yours, as some can be rooted in the subconscious mind where it is hard to detect.

One of Napoleon Hill's six basic fears is the fear of poverty. This fear he explained grew out of human beings preying on their fellow human beings. Through the fear of poverty, many have over worked themselves. Many, in their determination to be rich and avoid poverty, have worked at the expense of many other things. It has been said that the best way to help the poor is not to be part of them. I agree with this saying but suggest people do not avoid poverty at the expense of other things. Sadly, many are staying away from poverty at the expense of their health, family, and soul. With fear of poverty, some spend more time at work than they spend at home. The fear of poverty has led many to take actions that are detrimental to their progress and future.

The second fear identified by Hill is the fear of criticism. Many are afraid of being criticized that they would rather go with the flow. Criticism and fear of it has kept some people into inaction mode because of what people say. At the back of some worries and indecision is a form of fear. The fear of death is another form of fear. Many are kept from living due to this fear of death. Next is the fear of old age. Many businesses have gotten rich by preying on this fear. They come up with miracle pill, miracle cream and miracle surgery to make a person look ten years younger.

Next is the fear of ill health. Fear of ill health has driven many to ill health. Taking vitamins and having poly pharmacy that results in some medications interacting and in some cases becoming detrimental or fatal to their lives. Fear of loss of loved ones. This has seriously manifested in jealous love triangles where a person feels that instead of losing the loved one, they would rather hurt them to make them unattractive to others.

Transcending my fear gave me the doorway to achieve my freedom.

We had planned to travel to Nigeria for my father in law's burial. My husband had mentioned to me that we will be going together to Nigeria while the children stayed behind with the nanny. How can we travel together? What do you mean we are traveling together I asked him? I looked at him strangely, how come he does not get this? To a typical couple, it is fine to travel together. In fact, like the saying goes, the more the merrier. However, I was not seeing it that way. Unknown to me at the time, I was being driven by fear. I made many decisions out of fear.

If you had asked me then, I would have denied ever doing that. I was having a mastermind with some friends years later, and the whole truth came out. I learned on the mastermind about the six basic fears. I realized I had a big fear of death. My state of mind was operating under fear. I know, as a Christian I should not, but the fact was that at the time my child needed attention and full care, I was concerned about what could happen to him if am not here. I was operating under fear, refusing to travel in the same flight as my husband.

I would tell my children at the time that if anything ever happened to me, please do not put Lou in a nursing home. This fear was driving me so much that I took an additional million dollar insurance on my life. Yes, I did. I am not proud to share this but I just want to be open. As much as I do not want to talk about this, talking about it can be a blessing to millions. That was my fear then. Most people are fortunate if they do not suffer from the entire six. To get out of such trap of fear, I filled my life with power of faith to get me together again. Faith in God, faith in fulfilling my destiny, faith in myself, and faith in others.

Are you operating under any fear? Identify the six basic fears and ask yourself which one is yours. Be honest, because an enemy identified is enemy conquered. After I identified this enemy, I refused to be a slave to it. Many people operate under fear. Operating under any of these basic fears does not give the Inner Winner within chance to unleash. Identify yours and face that giant.

I taught myself never to use emotions to make decisions. Like the saying goes that fear is only false evidence appearing real. This is so true. Let faith guide you to pleasing your Maker. Never allow fear to overtake you. You must rise above all fears. Rising above your fear is cultivating the land before the seed gets planted in the soil. Be brave and face your fear. The brave eat their fear before their fear eats them.

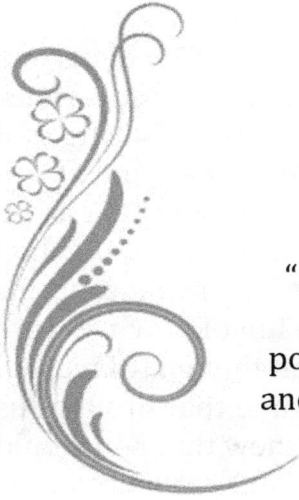

CHAPTER 3
Duty Calls in Another Continent

"If you want to feel connected to your own purpose, know this for certain: Your purpose will only be found in service to others, and in being connected to the something far greater than your mind/body/ego."
– Wayne Dyer

We were blessed to have angels in the form of people sent to take care of Lou. We had identified earlier that we will definitely need a live in nanny for Lou. So through word of mouth, we were introduced to Lisa, Lou's heaven sent nanny. Lisa was on assignment. An awesome person with a good heart, she truly cared for Lou. As much as Lou loved to eat, when fed, he would only take food from someone he loved. Lou may be very hungry, but if someone who did not love him tried to feed him, Lou would not open his mouth. When we met Lisa, Lou liked her instantly.

Although Lou was nonverbal, if carried by someone he loved, he would put his hands around that person's neck to signify friendship and acceptance. From the very first day Lou met Lisa, it was a perfect connection. We were fortunate to have her. Lisa was with us for 3 years. Eventually, she got married and had to move to another state. We all cried the day Lisa left. After Lisa, came parades of nannies to our home.

Many were not qualified to care for our Lou, they were just

after the money. When they come for interview, they distanced themselves from Lou, as if whatever Lou had was contagious. Oh, did we have parades of nannies in our home! During that time, my brother came to visit and saw how we were struggling with Lou. Yes it was a rough time for all of us. We lost a lot of our friends then, as our priority was to make our Lou comfortable. We are so thankful and grateful for that time, for it brought the best out of us all. We made fun of how we were all working shifts to take care of Lou. Even though it involved a lot of commitment, it was also a great time that brought us close as a family. Great because we never knew that Lou would die so soon, we gave our best, loved Lou and pampered him. We are so thankful for that time.

It was a time we looked back to when Lou died. We felt happy that Lou received our best the way we knew how. That period molded us, brought a lot of diamond out of us, opened up many doors and gave us divine promotion. It was the toughest challenge of our lives, yet it led to our biggest inspiration. We are so thankful that the trial time later qualified us for divine promotion because we had passed the test.

When my brother came on vacation, he saw all the challenges we had and how we worked shifts to care for Lou. He became really concerned. My brother notified mother about our shifts. Unknown to me, my mother had talked to my husband about taking Lou to Nigeria so we could move on with our lives. When I was asked, my answer was definitely not. Regardless of what package Lou came up as, he was my son and he wasn't going anywhere.

When my mother arrived in the USA, she did not even bother talking to me about taking Lou to Nigeria. Instead, she started working on my husband. My husband is a man of wisdom and was willing to see things from mother's perspective. After she won my husband over, she then started talking to my children.

I was living in my own world full of emotional decisions that I was not willing to compromise. A few days before mother went back to Nigeria, my mom, my husband and my children started talking to me about Lou going to Nigeria. I looked at everyone saying no, but I was so outnumbered.

The day Lou left for Nigeria was a very emotional day for all of us especially my daughter and I. Since we do not always know the men's emotions, my daughter and I were so sad that Lou was leaving. We cried, I was fortunate that the airline gave me a special pass to help my mom with Lou get on the plane. I cried like a baby praying that everyone change their minds and leave my son here with me. Needless to say, Lou went to Nigeria. At the time I was not too happy about it, but now I see the Hand of God was at work.

Lou had an assignment to do in Nigeria. He had lives to touch. I am so glad I did not use my selfish decision to stop Lou from completing his assignment. When Lou arrived in Nigeria, his second angel who was on assignment met him. Her name is Comfort, she connected with Lou right away.

Lou also received Comfort. They connected the very first time. Comfort gave Lou her best, took care of Lou, pampered Lou and loved Lou. I am so thankful to God for Comfort as she was God sent. For a long time, Lou would not allow anyone to feed him but Comfort.

Comfort was truly an angel. She loved Lou, took care of him day and night. Only God can reward her. Oh how she loved Lou. Even when my husband and I visited Nigeria, all we could say is thank you Lord.

CHAPTER 4
God's Angel Returns Home

"Good men must die, but death cannot kill
their names."
– Unknown

It has been said that the pen is mightier than the sword. This is so true. The Bible teaches in the book of 1 Corinthians chapter 10 that every test you have experienced is the kind that normally comes to people. But God keeps his promise, and he will not allow you to be tested beyond your power to remain firm; at the time you are put to the test, he will give you the strength to endure

> I know that God is too wise to be mistaken; He is too good to be unkind.

it, and so provide you with a way out. This is very empowering at the time of trouble.

Lou had lived in Nigeria for two years. Both my husband and I had visited Lou but we wanted him home with us. My husband and I agreed that Lou will come to New Jersey for two months. We got the ticket and started making preparations for Lou's arrival. Initially, we spoke of hiring a nanny for two months to help with Lou. But one day, I told the family that I chose to be home from work for those two months to take care of Lou.

We were all excited, buying Lou's favorite food, getting clothes, making plans, oh excitement was in the air. Lou's room was ready; everyone was ready for Lou's arrival. Unknown to us, it was never meant to be. However, the excitement and preparation really helped us in grieving for Lou. The preparations and excitement demonstrated our love and commitment to Lou. We are so thankful that no one complained or grumbled when we were preparing for Lou's arrival. That was our testing ground. Thank God we all passed.

Our peace is not dependent upon outward circumstances; it is dependent upon the God who dwells within us. Learn to wait and prepare because God is never late to promote. There is always a required time period of preparation prior to any season. An athlete who does not put himself through a physical training program will not be able to endure the season ahead. The same is true for you and I. Neglecting to prepare is actually preparation for failure.

Lou was to arrive with my mom on Friday. He died of respiratory failure Monday of the same week. Yes, Lou died a few days before we were to reunite again. I know that God is too wise to be mistaken; He is too good to be unkind. So on days I don't understand some situations, or when I do not see God's plans for my life in certain situations like this or even when I cannot trace God's Hands; such times, I have learned to believe and just trust God's heart. That is exactly what I did. Trust God even when the situation did not make sense.

The old adage is true. What does not kill you makes you strong. Lou is with the Maker, an extra angel watching over us. We are indeed thankful for his coming to this world. His life was short but very meaningful. To God alone be the glory. Moving forward, I promised myself not to blame the event, though it is a tragedy, my response to this situation will bless the world. I will not permit myself to worry about the things I cannot change. There, I began a journey of perseverance and trusting what God has in plans for me. Doubts, fear, worry, depression and all thoughts of limitation will not be permitted in my mind.

When friends came to offer their condolences, we were strengthened and empowered. We went to church the following day for service. Some friends who came to see us met our absence. I gave my icebreaker speech at my local toastmaster a few weeks later; there was no dry eye in the room. I later counseled some who had gone through some form of loss. In it all I saw purpose; I discovered fully my purpose from this incident. Indeed, the toughest challenge of my life led to my biggest inspiration. I became equipped to encourage, inspire and motivate millions.

With this tragedy, I discovered a great power within me. Living in faith helped me know that there is a solution to every problem. Even though it is an adversity, I had to find the seed of equivalent benefit that will help my family and I. I discovered that every great person met with adversity, failure and defeat. Though this situation hurts so much, I know that the dice of God is always loaded. There are goodies coming our way. I am blessed and thankful for God is good. The element of faith is the only sure power I have right now I said to myself. That I am holding on to.

CHAPTER 5
Life Without Lou

"May God bless you with enough foolishness
to believe that you can make a difference in
this word, so that you can do what others
claim is impossible."
– Franciscan Prayer

A caring mother will do absolutely anything for her child; I was no exception. I could not figure why Lou had to go through all these complications. As an adorable child, he was frustrated with being trapped. Oh the many lessons I learned from Lou. He was naturally calm; he had a lot of tolerance to pain. There was a time he fell and had a fracture from the fall, it was not noticed until days later. Oh poor Lou, he must have been in such pain. However, he was always quiet, calm and composed. I had zero tolerance to pain. Any little discomfort, I will yell and scream. Through Lou, I learned perseverance.

I used to be a queen of murmuring. I would murmur about anything not going my way. Lou had right-sided weakness. With every strength, he fought his condition. Sometimes out of frustration of being unable to do certain things, he would just scream. Many times when we put him in the bed, he used his strong side to get himself out of bed. Such times, maybe I put him in bed next to me to take a quick nap. By the time I opened my eyes, Lou was standing next to the bed staring at me. Those times, I yelled out in shock and Lou would startle and fall on the floor. Whenever we put Lou on the bed, he rolled till he got to the side of the bed and then just stood holding the bed. Lou was not able to stand independently so any time we saw this, we got concerned because we did not want

> "The LORD is a refuge for the oppressed, a place of safety in times of trouble."
> Psalms 9:9

him falling. These moments later came as a time we dearly wanted back. But sadly it never happened. As much as we wanted Lou to walk and be independent, it was always a concern seeing him by the side of the bed. After all these, Lou had a major incident that put him in coma for five days. This incident left him weak on both sides. It was a painful time for us all, but it was also the time the most transformation happened in all our lives.

The first pastor who connected with us concerning Lou is a friend. I was home one day, feeling really sad and crying, asking my Maker for wisdom to take care of Lou. Coincidentally, I received a call from a friend who at the time worked in Delaware. He said he had received prompting from God that he should call me. I was super excited that God sent me a message at a time that I was really desperate. God used the brother mightily for my family. He remains a friend until today.

It has been said that there are four types of people in our lives. The people who add to us, the ones who subtract from you, the ones who divide and the ones who multiply us. I was helpless, wanted answers, I needed wisdom to take care of my child. There came parades of users. I was vulnerable, a mother who was desperate to see the son healed. I came across some so-called users, pretending to be here to help.

They claimed to be praying for my son but never knew my son's name. They came alright and took advantage of my vulnerability. Every time they called to tell me they were praying for Lou was when they needed money. Oh those times! Some went as far as offering a concoction, which I refused. Some accused me that I was the cause of Lou being like that. They threw stones of accusations at me. I almost lost my mind but for the goodness of God.

I have to be open about all these not for self-pity, but more for whoever is going through a similar situation to know that you have to develop the Inner Winner within. You are a champion. You were not created for the situation to take over you. However, you must unleash your Inner Winner. Proxy people are a reality hiding under umbrellas of people of God. They actually represent the devil. People of God do not hit a fly with a hammer, people of God add value, they multiply. These ones came to subtract and divide; You must develop your relationship with The Maker. He alone will not fail you. I trusted, some I called my mentors, only for them to pull the carpet from under my feet. I fell, I was down, I did not have any option than to look up as my back was already on the floor. Only then did I discover and unleash the Inner Winner within.

Many stabbed me and left me bleeding. The same people I ran to for refuge gave me more pain. They hurt me, and hurt me bad. Now, I look back at such times, and I see perfection in them. The positive I got out of this situation is a gift, yes a gift of freedom. Instead of turning to man for answers, the hand of man only failed. God gave us that free will to choose.

At that time, I let emotions control my action, gave away my free will. Yes gave away my God given free will. Going to my Maker through proxy relationship. I am so glad the curtains to the temple were torn. All barriers between me and my Maker had to be broken.

If they had not disappointed me, such barriers would still be erected. What barrier is between you and the Creator? The barrier needs to be broken to connect with the Maker and unleash the Inner Winner within. I am thankful and grateful to God. Do not be addicted to man, maintain your God given free will and be connected to your Maker.

In the world, there is good and evil. I am thankful for the good. I also have some faithful people who are constantly praying even without notifying me. They prayed for my family and I, never asked me for a dime, for this I am eternally grateful. Christ will reward you. Once, Lou was in coma, this happened around the holiday season. Lou was in coma for 5 days. I sat at the intensive care unit with Lou and I refused to leave. At that time, I would rush to the bathroom and back. I told the hospital staff that when Lou wakes up, I want to be the first person he sees.

So I was glued to his bedside. By day 4, the nurses became seriously concerned about me. They told my husband he had to take me out; I refused. It became a big deal because they felt it was a psychological torture for me, so my husband persuaded me to leave. I realized that there was a night vigil in church. Night vigil is a Christian service where people pray all night. OK, that will work, I said. So I left the intensive care unit to go to night vigil. I needed divine intervention and the Lord met me big time. Oh how I am thankful to God for his loyal servants who seriously care for His children. The night vigil was to end, but the Pastor did not get OK spiritually to end night vigil. Eventually, I was called out and they prayed for me. The pastor did not even know what was going on in my life.

This is a church where no one knew what I was going through. But God identified me even out of the crowd. I am so thankful to God and am thankful to the servant of God who was available for The Master's use. Looking back at such times, I pray to God that I will also be an instrument of God's use to bring miracle to His children.

So to all who still put their salvation in men's hands, you have to stop being a man pleaser and be God pleaser. Stop chasing after men, you have a direct link with God, the curtains of the temple have been torn. There are no more barriers between you and your Creator. Go directly to your Maker. This is not to say that you cannot ask your pastors for prayer; yes you can. Stop running from pastor to pastor, stay with the shepherd of your fold and trust God for solution to what troubles you.

Remember that God is never intimidated by the circumstances you are going through. He alone has the solution in His hands. Be excited for the true testimony that whenever God is involved in a thing, He makes it better. God takes the pain and gives His power; takes our hurt and give us healing; takes our test and turns it into an international testimony; takes our failing and turns it to his success. So again I say, stop being a man pleaser and start being God pleaser. Have faith and seek Him diligently.

Lou is with the Maker now, and we miss him dearly. With God on our side all is well. Lou had to come teach me a lot, and now I am purpose driven. I have a lot of work to do, my purpose is to encourage, inspire, motivate and challenge millions. For what do you know about other people's bitter tears unless you have shed yours? I have shed my own tears and I have been comforted. Now, I am on a mission to comfort others. My passion is to add value to people's lives. I greatly desire that many reach their full potential regardless of what has happened to them in life. I love to give people a conscious interrupt! My guiding principle is that I don't seek to be better than others; I seek to be better than myself. I stay connected with God's lavish abundance so I continue to be a channel to radiate more of God's glory.

When I was born, the world rejoiced. I want to live my life leaving a timeless impact that will bless generations after me. Through an inner journey, I overcame struggles and re-occurring patterns and hence discovered the path to peace, success and freedom, I am qualified to touch many lives. I know that the toughest challenge of my life has led to my greatest inspiration.

My hope is that someday, I have the opportunity to meet you personally and to share the story of your success. The challenge that has brought the most tears to my eyes is the same reason the world is listening to me. Discern yours!

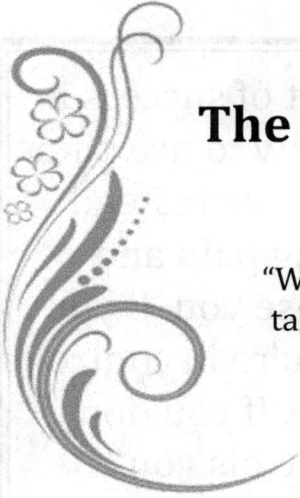

CHAPTER 6
The Inner Winner Unleashed

"We can let circumstances rule us or we can take charge and rule our lives from within."
– Earl Nightingale

You may have heard the saying that if the man is right, then his world will be right. You cannot always choose what happens to you in life since you are not always in control. You can however choose how you will respond to things that happen to you in life. Bad things have happened to many different types of people. Some of them have stayed bitter, depressed and gone on a downward journey while others in similar situations have used that negative situation as a stepping-stone to their success.

Staying in a place of hurt permanently is not the reason a person was created. You are a champion and have been created to shine like the stars, soar high like an eagle. You must decide you want to continue to soar to fulfill the reason for your creation, regardless of what life has thrown in your path. You are the missing puzzle in many lives; you have work to do and cannot allow yourself to be consumed in self-pity. You must reach that decision that regardless of what has happened to you, you must choose to move forward with life.

For me, the pit of sadness is monotonous, and I really did not want to continue to remain there. Part of my moving forward was to promise myself that I would observe my thoughts and entertain only those that empower me. Through this discovery, I committed to constantly learning and growing to discover more about

> "The secret of success is learning how to use pain and pleasure Instead of having pain and pleasure use you. If you do that, you're in control of your life. If you don't, life controls you."
>
> – Anthony Robbins

the mind and the way our thoughts work. If your mind and thought is not right, the outside world becomes shady.

During the toughest challenge of my life, I was in the pit, depressed and having a pity party. To start the journey out of these negative emotions, I used a lot of affirmations. I told myself, this Abiola, whose Maker is God, must get up as I have been destined to shine. Some of my affirmations are in the quotes chapter of this book. One day, I told myself, when you plant the seed of an apple, over time, an apple springs up from such seeds. What have I been planting in my mind I asked myself? As the aphorism that says " As a man thinketh in his heart, so he is." I had been sad over the challenges of Lou my eight-year-old son. That had filled my mind. I needed to replace this seed, but how do I do that? I have heard that my mind attracts whatever my mind dwells upon. At the time, I truly had attracted other negative things. Then, I thought why are people doing me bad? After all, they know what I was going through. In my self-examination, I realized what my mind has been dwelling upon and I needed urgent change. In making the needed change, I unleashed The Inner Winner.

One day, my mentor told me that I must know myself more. He went further to explain that winning in the game of life requires disciplining and training the mind. This resonated with me as I know that thoughts become things. He explained that on a daily basis, the picture held in my mind is creating my reality. The mind does not interpret positive or negative happenings. Meanings are in what you give. So if something happens to you, even if it is a negative happening, since you cannot change or do anything about it to reverse what has happened, you can choose to remain bitter in a pity party, or you can choose to learn from the experience and bring something positive out of a negative situation. I have read about Nick Vujicic, a man with no arms and no legs. Nick is now renowned for his work as an evangelist and motivational speaker. He is using his story and life to positively impact people. His message of faith and hope is blessing millions of lives all over the world. Indeed like the saying goes, facts tell and stories sell. For me, understanding how the mind works has helped me move on.

I am not an expert on mind psychology; I will only explain how the basic understanding of the mind has helped my life. I have moved on, also turned my toughest challenge to my inspiration, and in the

> "Fill your minds with those things that are good and that deserve praise: things that are true, noble, right, pure, lovely, and honorable."
>
> – Philippians 4:8

49

process, creating a life of significance that is blessing many.

Before I talk about the Inner Winner, let me explain more about the conscious and sub conscious mind. We all have one mind, and it is important to know how it works. The one mind can be divided to conscious and subconscious mind.

The conscious mind is our thinking. It is like going to a restaurant and placing the order for your food. The conscious mind is your order. It is the seed you plant in the soil as a gardener. The conscious mind sees things as true, it is where the world with or without lies. Whatever you impress to the conscious mind will be expressed by the subconscious. The conscious mind is where you have your logic and reasoning. It is where you do self-talk. The conscious mind is where you have your belief and accept decisions of life. It is your waking mind awake when you are. In your conscious mind, you can choose to have fear, worry, anxiety, hatred, discord, jealousy, fits of rage, selfish ambition, dissensions, factions envy, drunkenness and other negative emotions. On the other hand you can choose to have love, joy, peace, forbearance, kindness, goodness, faithfulness, gentleness and self-control. Since we are what we think, if you think garbage, you get garbage out.

The subconscious mind is your real self. It is the soil of your thought. The world within is your subconscious. Whatever has been impressed from the conscious mind is expressed from the subconscious mind. The subconscious mind is the kitchen that prepares the food you ordered in the restaurant. The subconscious mind cannot change the order of food. Whatever was ordered in the restaurant of the conscious mind is what the kitchen of the subconscious prepares and delivers. It is the soil that plants the seed from the conscious mind. So whether the seed is in form of negative emotions, or positive emotions, you get what you plant. The thought that has been sown from the conscious mind gets the reaction from the subconscious mind.

The subconscious mind deals with involuntary actions, emotions and visualization. The subconscious mind creates and executes ideas. It never sleeps, working 24 hours a day and 7 days a week. The purpose of our subconscious mind is to deliver what we want to us. One of the reasons we are encouraged to have positive emotions is because the subconscious mind picks up positive thoughts supported by positive emotions and delivers good things. When these emotions are negative, it carries out the same order. The subconscious mind cannot lie idle. You must instill positive thoughts into it, or it will feed on the thoughts that reach it as a result of your neglect.

You must understand that the same level of thought that has brought you this far will not be enough to take you to the next level. You must learn to master your thinking and direct your thoughts towards your desired result.

A deeper level of mind or thinking is what I call The Inner Winner. This is the treasure house of eternity within everyone. It consists of understanding of the conscious and subconscious mind at a higher level. The Inner Winner is a place with no limitation. It is where the external truth of life lies. It never changes. It has been said that we are spiritual beings having human experience. Going back to creation, the Bible teaches in Genesis 2 verse 7 that then the LORD God took some soil from the ground and formed a man out of it; he breathed life-giving breath into his nostrils and the man began to.

To understand The Inner Winner, you must know yourself. Most people are working on others and do not take time for themselves, always doing for others. The saying that we are human beings and not human doings is so right. Get ready to know yourself and discover the Inner Winner. Whenever you are traveling on a flight, before the plane takes off, you hear the following.

"In the event of a change in cabin pressure, panels above your head will open revealing oxygen masks. Pull the mask down toward you to activate the flow of oxygen. Cover your nose and mouth with the mask. Place the elastic band around your head and continue to breathe normally. Remember to secure your own mask before assisting others."

This is telling us to take care of ourselves first before taking care of others. The Bible says love your neighbor as yourself. Many people are trying to put other people's mask on first before putting theirs on. You must know yourself and be true to yourself. You must work on your imagination and not be a victim of distorted imagination. The Inner Winner is the mind of God; it is a human computer, the most magnificent machine made by only The Manufacturer Himself. This machine is another level of the mind.

Every seed in the form of thought sown in my mind becomes a seed that can take me to the next level or keep me in "why me?" mode. The mind if used correctly will serve you and work for you. It will teach you how to achieve goals and move forward with your life regardless of what has happened to you.

The Inner Winner is the Mind of God that dwells within all of us. This mind has the divine design for our lives. Even when the unexpected happens in our lives, the design is still intact. You must master your mind and emotions to get back on track.

You alone are the one who can fill and do that divine design. No one else, regardless of how much they love you. By the power of your will, you must be determined to unleash this Inner Winner. Many only go as far as the subconscious mind. Do not buy into the culture but go further and discover The Inner Winner where your life has a real purpose. Your Inner Winner gives you purpose and your divine destiny.

The Inner Winner is a place of spirituality where there are no limitations. The Bible says, "In Him we live and move and have our being. "You must master your emotions, as The Inner Winner cannot operate with negative emotions. Let positive emotions like love, joy, peace, forbearance, kindness, goodness, faithfulness, gentleness and self-control be what you hold in your mind.

When you are in the pit of life, The Inner Winner gives you solutions. Sometimes, when you hear the solution, it may not even make sense but following and applying it with faith will create for you the solution and extraordinary life. Many times, the Inner Winner has flashed solution to people's problems, but because they are stuck in negative emotions, they dismiss the solution, and say it is impossible. That explains the saying that looking eyes do not always see. Just like a seed is packed with power which when put in the right soil grows and multiplies, so also resides a power within.

My mentor with a full understanding of this tells me to write my goals down. Do not worry about how it will be done. In life, something will try to hold you down, yours is to resist it by following instincts and divine flashes, never stay in pools of problems complaining. Everyone that is living has problems; the only people who do not have problems are the people not living. You have absolute control of your mind. Know yourself. Take the time to connect with the Inner Winner.

Everything changes when you connect to The Inner Winner, once unleashed, you must never allow the voices of the world to drown the Inner Winner within. The Holy Spirit who dwells in all of us is our Inner Winner. The Holy Spirit will not force Himself on anyone, instead, we all have been given free will. The Inner Winner is waiting to connect with you, the Inner Winner is a silent listener waiting for your order. "Concerning the works of my hand, command you me". This is indeed so true, you must connect with The Inner Winner within. Discover the Inner Winner, where there is joy, perfection and completion.

CHAPTER 7
The Secrets That Changed My Life

"The fruit of the Spirit is love, joy, peace."
– Galatians 5:22

A change of feeling is a change of life. Abraham Lincoln once said it is in my observation that people are just as happy as they make up their minds to be. This is so true. Not making up your mind to be happy is making the decision not to be, so make up your mind and choose to be happy.

My coach invited me for a live event which was a big eye opener for me. In that live event, I saw the difference between achievers and underachievers. While ordinary people complain, murmur and talk about what they do not want, the successful focus on gratitude regardless of what is going on in their lives. At first I thought of course they have to be grateful because they have everything they need. Was I wrong? I discovered

> "Make your future dream a present fact, by assuming the feeling of the wish fulfilled."
> – Neville

that many have more problems than ordinary people, yet they focus on the opposite of what they are experiencing and focus on what they want. When you get close to them, some even walk around with headphones which I thought was strange. The headphones came in handy because when people around them say something that does not agree with them, they immediately put their headphones on. Some of them begin most of their sentence with "I am grateful and thankful". The lesson learned is that gratitude opens the door to more. I have always known this as a Christian that gratitude opens door for more, however, I also do murmur especially when things do not go my way. Now I saw continuous gratitude in action. Many other people talked about these men, they model their success by also saying they are thankful and grateful. Life is going to stop in different places, so be grateful about each stop. We have been given a gift in so many ways by God. We have to show appreciation for in our appreciation comes the duplication of good things happening. Never focus on the liability, focus on the assets of life for whatever you feed your mind will grow.

If you forget everything I have said so far, do not forget this secret to be grateful and thankful.

Another secret is that regardless of what is going on in your life, you must be happy. Even if you are in a tough situation, use that situation for your direction. It is through what you are going through that your strength is developed. The day my son died was the saddest day of my life. I remember my pastor saying to me not to be sad, I was told to play gospel music and be happy and trust God. I could not do that I thought. How can I play gospel music when am sad I asked? Not long after that I took the advice, because my being sad attracted more sad thoughts.

I needed to escape from that pity party. Happiness is a key that will unlock many doors for you. You must be happy, everything you want will give you happiness. If that is the case, you need to be happy now to attract what you want. You have heard several times that your inner world creates your outer world, so be happy now, you cannot afford to forget that. You must attract happiness and joy, move beyond previous hurt and disappointment. I used to be an unconscious incompetence about this secret till I became aware of the many doors happiness can open, and became unconscious competence.

I was listening to one of my mentors when he mentioned the following exercise. He asked me if I would rather have a million dollars given to me right now or a penny doubled every day for the next thirty days. The thought of a million dollars right now excited me. Knowing who my mentor is, he expected me to think twice before I answer. After thinking with a quick calculation in my head, I told him I would rather have a million dollar right now, the things I could do with that. I started dreaming of possibilities. It surprised me that by waiting patiently for 30 days, I would end up with $10,737,418.

In today's life of instant gratification, persistence is not a skill many have, yet this skill is very important to get to the next level. The beginning of change is like a rocket ship that is taking off into space, it spends 80% of fuel during take off, but afterwards, flies with minimum fuel. So with persistence, your efforts will pay dividends. Make a penny's worth of investment in yourself. The compound interest in every penny investment will be worth millions if you are persistent and don't give up.

Regardless of what has happened to you, come to that moment of decision where you choose to be happy. You can do the 30 day challenge like you were offered a penny doubled every day for the next thirty days. Even though we live in a world of instant gratification, you will be persistent for thirty days after which you will become unconsciously competent. To begin the journey, drop the pity mindset of what happened to you like you are the first person in the world this happened to. You must also drop the mindset of the world owing you things because the world does not does not owe you anything. Dropping such a mindset helps you prepare for the journey we are about to embark on.

CHAPTER 8
There Is Much Hope

"May God, the source of hope, fill you with all
joy and peace..."
– Romans 15:13

Life's challenges are not supposed to paralyze you; they are supposed to help you discover who you really are. Do not let the past hold you hostage, or color your future. Every major difficulty you face in life is like a fork on the road, you alone can decide what turn you want to go, through bitterness or greatness. You must move on and you can do it.

Our hopes, our desires, our motivation, our inspiration makes us human. Do not lose hope, you cannot afford to lose hope. We all came to this world with a blank book, nothing written on it. Every day of our lives new experiences are recorded, page by page as we go through life. Sometimes, there are experiences that we do not like but we cannot get stuck on a page. We cannot close the book saying it will never be open again. The book is not completed; it gets completed only when we die. Regardless of what has happened to you in life, we have to reflect, evaluate the experience and move on.

Never let the experience make you bitter, instead allow it to make you better. You cannot change what happened to you, however, you can change where you are heading to and what the experience will do in you. In life, we all experience more than what we understand. Too much happens that we sometimes cannot explain. The best way to move forward is to make the best of what you can understand.

Christ gave an open invitation for all those who labor and are heavily laden to come to Him. Sometimes, even people who already have a relationship with Christ still carry unnecessary burden. Take Christ's offer and let Him give you rest, refuse to stay in the place of hurt. Staying on the battlefield of pain alone does not help you get out of pain. Take it to your Maker where victory is guaranteed.

Many of God's goodies are sent daily to us. Discover your Inner Winner and unleash. Hope is real so please do not waste your life worrying over what you cannot change. There is much hope.

Life dealt my son some heavy blows. When I think about it, I used to get really upset and do the pity party where I was the only one attending. Lou could not see, he could not talk, he could not walk, he could not... and the list was endless. Lou's diagnosis was unknown. I remember how my husband and I went to so many doctors to find out what was wrong with Lou.

One day, his neurologist, another God sent angel, told us not to waste our time looking for a diagnosis. From a medical diagnosis, this may be

> "I alone know the plans I have for you, plans to bring you prosperity and not disaster, plans to bring about the future you hope for."
>
> – Jeremiah 29:11

unknown, and your son does not fit in any diagnosis that we know. That was a wake-up call for my husband and I, for before then, we had gone to so many doctors who only upset us more. I remember an experience where this so called specialist sat across the table and stared at Lou's paper work and Lou without even standing to see Lou,

> "Nothing is predestined. The obstacles of your past can become the gateways that lead to new beginnings."
> – Ralph Blum

only to tell us to take him home and make him comfortable. Those where challenging times which brought my husband and I even closer together.

The whole situation taught me to hope. I learned to rejoice in hope, be patient in tribulation and constant in prayer. Hope taught me to discover and unleash The Inner Winner within and not compete with the opinion of everyone else. I reminded myself that I will let my dreams be bigger than my fear and through my hope; I will live by choice and not by chance. It was a deep pain, but it empowered me and gave me significant opportunities for growth and success, for it forced me out of my comfort zone.

Every true champion knows seasons of loneliness and being down. Moses must have known seasons of insignificance alone in the desert. David must have felt disconnected from the success his brothers enjoyed while he watched over the sheep. Christ must have felt very lonely and rejected carrying the sins of the world alone on the cross. You are not alone; God is with you!!!

It is so true that the school of life offers many lessons. Some of them we sign up for, some just happen without asking for our permission. In it all there are valuable lessons to learn and grow from if we do not stay bitter.

In the journey of life, there are ups and downs, detours and digressions, twist and turns, we must learn to hope and trust in our Maker. For anyone who has travelled in planes, you may have experienced a bumpy ride because of turbulence. The plane begins to jerk and you hear the captain's voice announcing that there is unexpected turbulence in the air. Turbulence does not care about the size of a plane, for it will shake any plane. The passengers are advised to take their seats and fasten their seat belt. So is life, you cannot do anything about the turbulence, but you can hope it stops and many times it does. No matter where you are in the journey of life, take hope that the best is yet to come. The road may be rough, the doors may seem shut, you may think there is no way out, but what does God say? "Behold, I will do a new thing; now shall it spring forth; shall ye not know it? I will even make a way in the wilderness and rivers in the desert".

Move on with your life and do not let the past hold you hostage. Be encouraged my friends for God will SURELY make a way!!!!

THE END ...

THIS IS REALLY THE BEGINNING FOR YOUR NEW ACTIONS

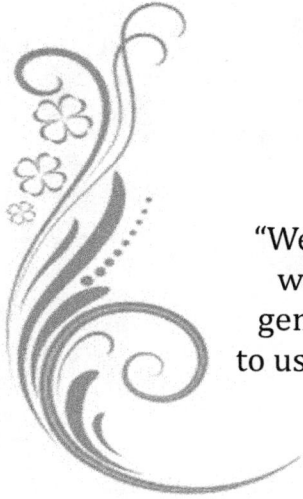

CHAPTER 9
Develop An Action Plan

"We should so live and labor in our time that what came to us as seed may go to the next generation as blossom, and that which came to us as blossom may go to them as fruit. That is what we mean by progress."
– Henry Ward Beecher

YOUR CURRENT REALITY
Starting Right now, I am making the decision to:

Write a list of the negative emotions you currently have to let go.

Negative emotions Rate 0-10 SCORE YOURSELF

FEAR

ANGER

GREED

HATRED

REVENGE

FRUSTRATION

BLAME

COMPLAINING

How do you plan to move on?

Write a prayer asking God to strengthen you as you move on.

Remember a time you experienced God's Grace and strength when you felt you could not carry on.

What are you hoping for?

Do you have a relationship with God?

A year from now, what would you like people to celebrate with you?

Identify some positive emotions you desire to move on.

Grade yourself 0 to 10, 0 being poor and 10 being very good, at the different dimensions of life. How well are you doing?

SPIRITUALITY

FINANCIAL

CAREER

SOCIAL

HEALTH

MIND

PERSONAL GROWTH

Whatever goals you have, go ahead and write those things down. Though it tarries, wait for it to manifest because it will surely come to pass (Habakkuk 2:2-3).

Now set goals to move you forward with your life.

GOAL SETTING EXERCISE
Set a SMART goal that is:

SPECIFIC: Your goal must be specific.

MEASURABLE: Real time measurable goals that are not vague.

ACHIEVABLE: Set goals you know you can achieve. It becomes easier to go after the goal because it is achievable.

REALISTIC: Setting an unrealistic goal is a setup for failure.

TIME BASED: What time do you want to achieve your goals? (Prevents procrastination)

1. State your end goal to achieve your life purpose and unleash The Inner Winner by the end of the year in the different dimensions of your life.

A.

B.

C.

D.

E.

F.

G.

2. What factors make this goal important to you?

3. List out the steps you need to take to accomplish the goal (E.g. things you need to do or learn? People you need to meet? Places you need to go?)

4. Hold yourself accountable to the following:

5. What did you gain or learn from reading this book?

6. How do you plan to pay it forward and bless someone else with this book or lesson learned?

7. From today, I commit to

You must move your life from a place of living, to a place of success, to a place of significance!

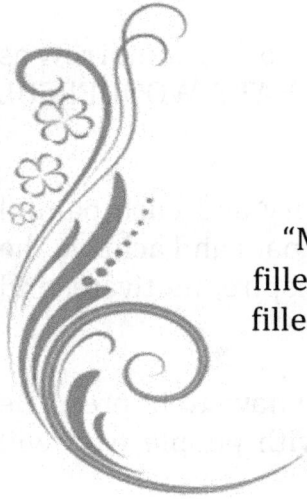

CHAPTER 10
Quotes by Abiola Saba

"My deepest hope is that rather than being filled with sadness over my loss; I want to be filled with inspiration that will create significance in millions of lives."
– Abiola Saba

When I was born, the world rejoiced. I want to live my life leaving a Timeless Impact that will bless generations after me.

The challenge that has brought the most tears to my eyes is the same reason the world is listening to me. Discern yours.

One of my greatest wishes and desire is to be the right person in other people's lives. When someone looks back years from now, and says: "One of the reasons for my success is that I met Abiola".

What do you know about other people's bitter tears, unless you have shed your own? I have shed mine and I have been comforted. Now I am on a mission to encourage, inspire, motivate and challenge others!!!

I was not born qualified but I have become qualified. From tragedy to triumph. Just when I thought I could not face tomorrow, He gave me hope and several reasons to face tomorrow as well as equipped me to help millions. O WHAT A WONDERFUL SAVIOR!

Each successful person has a painful story and each painful story has a successful ending. Accept the pain and achieve the gain. I am on a journey to encourage, inspire, motivate, and challenge millions to righteousness!!!

Stop spending your time with people you have to impress. Be true to yourself and spend your time with people who will bring the best out of you.

The toughest challenge of my life has led to my biggest inspiration.

Some people's words build bridges while others have words that build walls. Walls or bridges, you are planting seeds of success or failure in other people. Life is a boomerang; whatever you send out you will receive in multifold.

Never stop wrong people from leaving your life. For when they leave, wrong things stop happening.

The Champion in you cannot come out while you are in a palace or at a five star hotel. The champion comes out in your challenges. So accept the pain and move on with the gain to get to the palace.

Give your Inner Winner a chance to direct your calendar.

Do not let fear and limitations affect you from reaching the palace. Work on changing your mindset.

I am on a mission, to encourage, inspire, motivate and encourage millions to unleash the inner power within.

Be careful, how you shut the door in anger. You may need to go in again through that same door. Do not let anger direct you.

You never know what will motivate or move us to bigger, better things. If you have enjoyed this book, I would love for you to pass it on to your friends.

About Abiola Saba

Abiola Saba is an entrepreneur, speaker, trainer, coach, mentor and founding partner with the John Maxwell team. Abiola has a passion for God, compassion for people and through her coaching, speaking, and mentorship programs, she is committed to pursuing, proclaiming and publishing God's words for many to be successful and achieve their maximum potential.

Abiola greatly desires that many reach their full potential. As a trainer, she shares inspiration and motivational leadership to executives and leaders who in turn influence their organization. Abiola encourages over eleven thousand people through her daily inspiration on Facebook. She mentors and coaches many all over the world. Her guiding principle is seeking not to be better than others, but herself. She stays connected with God's lavish abundance so she can continue to be a channel to radiate more of God's glory.

Abiola is married to Mr. Ayo Saba and they are blessed with children. She resides with her husband in South Jersey.

Services Available

For more information call us today at 856-264-4480 or email saba@abiolasaba.com. Find out about:

. Keynote Speeches
. Coaching
. Mentorship
. Training Programs
. Personal Development
. Leadership Development

Looking for a Speaker?
If you are interested in having Abiola speak to your group or organization about:

. Leadership
. Teamwork
. Time management
. Goal setting
. Performance
. Personal development

Contact her for availability at the number and email listed above.

Leadership & Team Training

As a John Maxwell-certified trainer on Leadership, we offer the following programs, which can be adjusted to suit your needs and budget.

- Lunch and Learn Series Leadership Gold
- Put Your Dreams to the Test
- Becoming A Person of Influence
- The 21 Irrefutable Laws of Leadership
- Job Performance Wheel
- Everyone Communicates, Few Connect
- How to Be A REAL Success
- The 15 Invaluable Laws of Growth

Contact Abiola for:

- Keynote speeches and conventions
- Group coaching
- Personal life coaching
- Masterminds
- Training
- Lunch and Learn
- Church leadership empowerment
- Half-day and full-day workshops/seminars
- In-house corporate training
- Executive and personal retreats
- Team building

You Are A Champion!

I can see everything turning around for your good!

www.ingramcontent.com/pod-product-compliance
Lightning Source LLC
Chambersburg PA
CBHW060419050426
42449CB00009B/2034